**Th**

# Book of Comm

By William S. Frisbee Jr.

**TAB01**

*Acknowledgements:*

I would like to thank my wife for putting up with me and my hobbies, and the brothers that shoot at and with me.

For more information and discussions see the following:

**www.TheAirsoftBible.com**

**Check out Facebook at**

www.facebook.com/TheAirsoftBible/

The author's website is at
www.WilliamSFrisbee.com

# Table of Contents

## Contents

# 1.    Foreword

*"Common Sense isn't so common."*

  This book should not be a replacement for proper research OR for *using your freakin' brain* OR for *personal experience*. This book is not the ONLY way to do things. It is not the only RIGHT way to do things. In most cases it is one of several ways to do things. Sometimes it is one of several ways to do things WRONG. Although called a bible, it is a GUIDE, designed to help provide a basic understanding and grounding so that you can understand and adapt to YOUR situation. This book is not gospel, it is not the unquestionable bible, and it will not keep you from making mistakes. It is not going to make you the ultimate, uber-warrior and it will not answer all your questions. It should make you ask more questions and allow you to focus your research. It should help provide you with a box to think outside of.

  Why write this book? People sometimes think that they are failing to excel at airsoft (or paintball) because their weapon is not better, or their gear is not better, or their camouflage is not superior, etc. The reality is that their tactics *suck*. It is always easier to blame others. "I got shot because his weapon has a better range..." No, you got shot because he saw you BEFORE you got into range for your weapon. "I need a weapon with an insane rate of fire." That depends on why you really want the ROF. If you are a rifleman it is because you are a really bad shot and fifty rounds will increase your chance to hit. However, you look at it, somebody wearing Bermuda shorts and a Hawaiian shirt and using a springer pistol can defeat the 'uber warrior' with every weapon and piece of gear imaginable if Bermuda boy has superior tactics.

  I do not claim to know everything, be perfect or never make mistakes. Combat, even simulated combat like Airsoft, is an art form. Like all art forms there are many ways of doing things, many different schools of thought and many different techniques based on those schools. Airsoft and paintball are the same. Different people have different experiences that shape their perceptions and beliefs and different techniques work for different people, but not always for everyone.

The purpose of this book is not to be an end-all 'this is the only right way to do things' type book. It is designed to help people along the path of a Zen Airsoft Warrior. Everything in this book is intended to help guide warriors, **not** dictate to them. Every situation is different, every person is unique (just like everyone else,) so the real warrior should adapt to the situation and should not blindly follow dogma because it will inevitably be run over by Karma. The primary purpose of this book is to expand thinking and present new ideas and in some cases to give old ideas an additional look. The most effective warrior is one who can think for himself and adapt different techniques to the situation at hand. I will repeat myself in different areas to "hammer it home" or emphasize something.

As a former Marine infantry squad leader and a veteran, I think 'The Book' is a good teaching guide, but in reality, it is just a guide. It gives people a common frame of reference so that WHEN the script changes, people are more able to understand how and why it changed.

Professionals are predictable, but the world is full of amateurs. So, leave 'luck' to the amateurs and stack the deck in your favor.

Do not take this book as gospel. Read it, seek to understand it and use what works for you!

Thank you and Semper Fi
- William "Warcat" Frisbee

Aaron Thomas aka "Scorpion", Eric Webb aka "Logikal" and
Ryan Fenton aka "Fenton"

# 2.    Overview

Teamwork is essential. It gives the enemy someone (besides you) to shoot at. It keeps the enemy looking the other way while you get in that epic multiple kill. Communication is the key to teamwork. Even if you are using the rest of your team as BB fodder, there has to be communication. Either they communicate what they are doing and you take advantage of their, um, 'skill', or you work together with them as a lethal fighting force to crush your opponents.

When communication breaks down, the battle devolves into chaos and confusion. Initiative is lost and the firefight becomes everyone for themselves. Most open plays are like this.

What sets elite squads and teams apart from the mob is their ability to communicate and plan. A squad that is talking constantly among themselves, telling each other where the enemy is, what they are doing, what areas need to be covered, what has happened and what is going to happen is a very effective force. They are hard to surprise and able to mass their firepower in a decisive manner when it matters.

There are several ways to communicate; talking, radios, hand arm signals, hand signals, touch, whistles, Christmas cards, winks, e-mail, the grapevine, wolf calls, cell phones, pagers, horns, bugles, smoke signals, bag pipes, etc. The goal of communication is to convey information to a fellow quickly and effectively without also communicating it to the enemy.

A human wearing goggles can only see a small portion of the battle field, especially when that person is hunkered down behind a tree. It is nearly impossible to get a full perspective of the battle if all you can see is that small little slice. The more people there are, the more of the battle field there is that can be seen and understood, but only if those people can communicate what they see and hear to each other!

As the team communicates with each other about where the enemy is and where the enemy ISN'T, people can begin to exploit the weaknesses in the enemy formation - and there will *always* be weaknesses. This applies on the local firefight level as well as the strategic battle field level. The more people that can 'see' and understand, the more effective their decisions and actions will be.

With alarming frequency, I see players allow their friends to wander into the enemy line of fire because a friend or ally did not communicate that the enemy was there or had a clear field of fire in that area. As I said, there are several methods of communication that I will discuss in depth.

## 2.1. What to Communicate

Before I go into types of communication, I will cover what needs to be communicated in most cases. This is the part that most people screw up - with either too much, too little, or completely irrelevant information.

The military has a term "SALUTE" that is used for communicating information and intelligence information. This is great for reporting to commanders, but is not always relevant for most players.

Always take a second or two and think before you communicate if you can. This sounds like common sense, but when adrenaline is flooding your system, when you've been running, becoming one with the ground or otherwise distracted, it makes a difference. The best communicators sound like they are bored or still lying in bed. They are clear and brief, their speech is unhurried and almost monotone.

This is where communication becomes an art form.  The master of the art provides the most important information first and then proceeds to give supporting and other relevant information.  For example, "Enemy moving north to south, fifty meters to our front," is great.  *If* the listener knows where your front is and which way is north.  One key thing to remember is that if the listener has to figure out what you are telling him then there is a chance the listener will screw it up and misunderstand you.  When the adrenaline is flowing and twenty different things are happening, trying to figure out which way is north requires additional mental processing time.  "Two tan riflemen in the building to my front," sounds good, but what if there are three buildings in front of you?  Then the listener has to guess which one is to your front, which requires knowing exactly where you are.

You get the picture.  Everything is relative and this is where practice and familiarity (aka experience) comes in.  Always put yourself in the shoes of the listener.  Always try to make things as crystal clear as possible.  And always take a second to think about and mentally compose your message, especially if you are talking on the radio.  Never assume the listener knows.

When talking with someone, always try to use landmarks or quickly identified objects. "Center building", "Fallen Log", "Lighting cut tree", "Dead bush", "Bridge to staging area",  a player's name, etc.  Practice painting an accurate picture in as few words as possible. Next, describe what is happening.  "Exchanging

Fire", "Moving quickly", "Assault formation", etc. Then quickly describe any special actions you are taking or about your situation, "Sending a team to the left to flank", "Pulling back", "We are suppressed", "Not in any danger", etc. Once the critical items are covered, you can break it down with more information.

When talking, yelling, or using non-verbal communication (hand arm signals), always try to repeat it for your fellows, especially the non-verbal ones (hand arm signals). The original speaker or signaler might not be loud enough or visible to people further out in the formation so repeating it makes sure that everyone understands.

## 2.2. Here are some forms of communication

### 2.2.1. Radio

When one starts talking about communication, this is what most people think. Radios communication can be the most effective method and the most complicated. Unlike a phone, only one person can talk at a time and there are usually several people on the radio net.

### 2.2.2. Hand Arm Signals

Not everyone has a radio and sometimes the enemy might hear you when you are talking on it. Hand arm signals are quiet and effective, can be used over long distance, but only work when people are within sight of each other and of course, actually LOOKING at each other.

### 2.2.3. Hand Signals

Sometimes hand *arm* signals are too obvious, especially when hunkered down behind a tree or when you are very close to the enemy. Hand signals can be used to convey information quickly and quietly. They also require line of sight and the users to be looking at each other. In most cases, hand signals augment hand ARM signals instead of replacing them.

### 2.2.4. Talking

This is the most common form of communication, from yelling to whispering, it is what we have all been doing since we were knee high to a garden gnome. This does not require you see the person you are talking to and it does not require that they are looking at you. It does, however, reveal your presence and intent if the enemy is nearby and within earshot.

### 2.2.5. IFF – Identification; friend/foe

Newsflash - the other guys speak the same language you do! At night, in poor visibility conditions, or in thick vegetation, it is always nice to know whether you are about to engage in a close-range firefight with your friends or preferably with your enemies. There are several quick ways to get that other person to identify himself quickly and effectively without giving yourself away and/or exposing yourself.

## 2.2.6. Other Methods

Whistles, wolf howls, flashlights, clackers, hoots, farts, e-mail, touching, and hissing are other methods that can be used to get people's attention and convey information.

# 3.   Radio Communications

## 3.1. Overview

Radios are a great voice saver and can let you communicate quickly, reliably and relatively quietly over long distances. They are crucial at the strategic (in this case battle field) level and at the more immediate tactical (firefight) level. It is not practical to try yelling at someone fifty yards away, especially in the middle of a firefight. And rarely does using a radio give away your position, with the exception of CQB or really thick vegetation.

Before the game begins, the units should establish a communication plan. Decide upon radio channels and call signs. Radio checks should also be conducted. The best method of doing a radio check is to say something like, "Warcat Radio Check" (using your own name), or you can call someone else's name. The correct response is "Warcat you are loud and clear," or "Lima Charlie" or "Licken Chicken" or "Lumpy Coco" or anything else that starts with an "LC" for loud and clear. If the caller is NOT loud and clear, tell them. "You sound like you have gravel in your mouth, adjust your mic location" etc. This also gives the listener a chance to adjust their volume so they are not deafened.

Be very cautious of "hot mic-ing". This is when some bozo accidently jams their push-to-talk button and begins to jam the airwaves with their heavy breathing, unaware that they are transmitting. This also occurs when some brainchild puts their radio on VOX.

You should NOT use VOX for this reason. VOX stands for "voice initiated transmitting." When you start speaking, your radio starts transmitting. VOX usually starts transmitting when the noise level reaches a certain level. This means that when you start breathing heavily, you transmit. When you shoot, you transmit. When you start screaming you are hit, you transmit. When you clear your throat, you transmit. If you fart loud enough, you transmit. You trip and fall, you transmit, etc. This will make you very unpopular and soon you will find yourself on you own personal channel with nobody to talk to. It also takes a second to activate, meaning that you may be cutting off the first part of your transmission.

## 3.2. Radios

### 3.2.1. Radio Operations\Communications

Radio communications should be short, sweet and to the point. Operators should minimize unnecessary communications as much as possible. If you want to discuss the weather, last night's football game or how great you are then you shouldn't be allowed to use a radio and should probably be sent to a channel all by yourself. If you do discuss these things on the radio during a game then you should be used for SAW target practice.

Trivia devotees will note that unlike a cell phone, only one person can talk at a time on a radio. So if you are wasting time jabbering like a fool on the radio then nobody else can talk or tell you about that flanking force coming up behind you. More professional players will change channels, or turn their radio down or off so that they don't have to deal with you. When you need help you can know with confidence that nobody is listening.

When speaking, you should first take a breath and calm down. People will not understand you if you are yelling, panting, or talking too fast. The best radio communicators sound like they are terribly bored and sitting behind a desk or still laying in bed. **Remain cool and calm!** *Think* about what you are going to say before you say it on the net.

There are many different ways of doing things in radio communications. What I describe here is usually the method I prefer, but I have included some alternates as well.

**Initiating Communications:** This is best done by saying the other person's call sign **twice** and then yours. For instance, "MechEng, MechEng, this is Warcat". Listeners may not hear the first name said (in this case MechEng), but by the 2nd saying of their name are usually listening in time to hear who is calling them, or their buddy next to them will clue them in.

Some people like the "Warcat calling MechEng" method, but I have found that the listener might not always know who is calling them. When people are concentrating on something else (like somebody shooting at them) their attention is not focused on the radio and they may have to turn their attention back to the radio to be effective.

**Commonly heard terms;**

"**Over**" - helps the listener understand that the speaker is waiting for a response.

"**Out**" - helps the listener(s) understand the speaker is done with the communication and moving on to other things.

"**SitRep**" - is a request for a situation report.

"**How Copy**" - is a request from the speaker to the listener asking if the listener understands. This is a request for a brief back.

"**Hard Copy**" or "**Solid Copy**" - indicates that the listener understands fully but doesn't feel like repeating it. Or it might be used by the originator of a message to indicate the brief back was good.

"**Say Again (your last)**" - is a request for the last speaker to repeat the last transmission. Do NOT use the word "repeat" as it is considered very bad form (and is actually a command to repeat an artillery or mortar fire mission).

"**Please advise**" - is a request for orders.

"**Break**" - is used when the speaker needs to take a breath and should be done frequently to give others a chance to break into the net in the event of an emergency. This can also be used if someone needs to break into a conversation by repeating "break" several times.

However, "flash" is more appropriate for breaking a conversation.

**"Correction"** - means that the message was not repeated properly and should be followed by the correct information.

**"Disregard"** - means that the information that was about to be shared is obsolete or incorrect.

**"Roger"** - is not someone's name so much as an acknowledgement that the order was received. This is not used much anymore now that people are actually named Roger.

**"Wait"** - means to wait for a few seconds while the speaker talks with someone, gets more information or finishes a task.

**"WILCO",** is army terminology for "WILL Comply" – and means that the message has been received and will be acted upon. Don't use "roger wilco" as this is redundant and a radio communication faux pas.

**"Flash, Flash, Flash", "Silence on the Net",** or **"Radio Dark"** - means silence on the net. All units maintain radio silence while important information is shared or a high priority transmission is resolved. Only higher authorities are authorized to give these commands.

**"Resume Normal Traffic"** - indicates that the "Flash, flash, flash", "Silence on the Net", or "Radio Dark" condition is lifted.

### 3.2.2. Reports

There are a couple types of report formats that can be used on a radio to communicate information to higher command or other team members.   For the most part, the following reports are used.

## Contact Report

This is a critical report for higher level commanders and should not be ignored. The report is given the second rounds are fired OR the enemy is observed whenever possible and should include the following information:

**WHO** – Who is calling.

**WHAT** – What is happening, taking fire, sighted the enemy, ambush initiated, etc.

**WHERE** – Where the unit is located.

**ACTIONS** – Estimated actions

Once those four items are transmitted it is expected that a full SALUTE report will follow shortly thereafter.   The contact report is a quick warning to higher command that you are about to step into 'it' and if they don't hear from you again they can mark on their map, "Here there be dragons."

## SALUTE Report

This is a more detailed report and applies to enemy forces. It is very structured to help give other people a better grasp on the situation and enemy troop deployment. This can be given at any time, before, during or after the fight. It is usually better to give it as soon as possible in case you get killed. You do not have to give ALL the information. It should be expected that you do not know everything, but the goal here is to at least GUESS what you are up against. You can always correct the report later, but if you get killed then nobody will know anything.

S – Size of the enemy force

A – Activity of the enemy force. What are they doing, where are they going, how they are deployed.

L – Location of the enemy force

U – Uniform or Unit. This should be obvious, but if they are one of the established squads this is good information to pass on.

T - Time that contact was made

E – Equipment. Do they have any special weapons, boxes, equipment or gear?

## Ammo Casualty Report

This report is simple and you just let your commander know if you are running out of ammo or have a large number of casualties. This report is sent AFTER the firefight so the commander knows you are still alive and the condition of your unit.

### 3.2.3. Phonetic Alphabet

The purpose of the phonetic alphabet is to make sure letters and numbers are properly understood over a radio where static, accent, background noises or speaker stress may affect pronunciation. For example " 'C' Company" might sound like " 'G' Company" on the radio.

A – Alpha

B – Bravo

C – Charlie

D – Delta

**E** – Echo
**F** – Foxtrot
**G** – Golf
**H** – Hotel
**I** – India
**J** – Juliet
**K** – Kilo
**L** – Lima
**M** – Mike
**N** – November
**O** – Oscar
**P** – Papa
**Q** – Quebec
**R** – Romeo
**S** – Sierra
**T** – Tango
**U** – Uniform
**V** – Victor
**W** – Whiskey
**X** - X-ray
**Y** – Yankee
**Z** – Zulu

Number pronunciation is a way to pronounce numbers over the radio so they are clearly understood by a listener.

**0-** Zeero
**1-** Wun
**2-** Too
**3-** Tree or Thr-ree
**4-** Fower
**5-** Fife
**6-** Siks or Sex
**7-** Seven

**8-** Ate

**9-** Niner

### 3.2.4. Call Signs

A call sign is NOT a screen name. Call signs should be short, sweet and to the point. Someone with a call sign like "Wearer of fluffy bunny slippers", "Sniper777413" or "Son of Liberty" will be asked to use a different radio channel that everyone else will conveniently 'forget' or 'lose' while neglecting to share their own channel.

Numbers with call signs are frequently used to denote a position or team, but should be short.

Two or three syllable call signs (that are easy to pronounce) are best. They should roll off the tongue and be easily understood on the radio. Apache, Comanche, Headshot, MechEng, Warhawk, ToeJam, Rumcake, Princess, Bigfoot, and 404 are good examples.

In some cases a platoon or squad may be assigned a call sign, for instance "Apache". Then based on standard procedures, elements within that unit take on additional 'call signs'. This can vary between units and branches so it should be discussed beforehand.

**&lt;call sign&gt; actual** is the unit commander, not the RTO. (Marine Speak)
**&lt;call sign&gt; six** may also refer to the unit commander (Army speak)
**&lt;call sign&gt; one** is the 1$^{st}$ team, squad, platoon, or company.
**&lt;call sign&gt; two** is the 2$^{nd}$ team, squad,

platoon or company.

**<call sign> one actual/six** would be the platoon or company commander instead of the RTO.

**<call sign> five** is the company XO.

**<call sign> seven** is the company first sergeant.

**<call sign> two one** could be 2nd squad, 1st Fireteam.

Another method to identify a unit is with numbers denoting platoon and squad. For instance, "Apache Wun-Wun" would be Apache Company, 1st Platoon, 1st Squad. "Apache Wun-Too" would be Apache Company, 1st Platoon, 2nd Squad, etc.

Whatever is decided, it should be short and very simple. Leave the complexity to the people who do it for a living and usually establish their own standard operating procedures.

## 3.2.5. Call Signs for Locations and Objectives

While it can get confusing sometimes to assign call signs to objectives or locations it makes good sense tactically. Inevitably, the enemy has the ability to 'listen in' on conversations. When the order is given to a subordinate unit for instance to attack the enemy HQ, an enemy listening in then knows to reinforce their HQ or to move it. When a subordinate unit is directed to attack "Hotel Quick" then the enemy is left to wonder. One method that makes it easier to remember what is what is to just change the names, not the initials.

For instance "Gold City" becomes "Groovy Cow" and "HQ" becomes "Happy Queen", etc.

### 3.2.6. Example Conversations

## Enemy Sighting (Good Example)

*"Bigfoot, Bigfoot this is RumCake, come in."* - RumCake wants Bigfoot to wake up and start listening.

*"This is Bigfoot, go."* – Bigfoot wants to know 'Whadya want'.

*"You have an enemy squad approaching you from the North, they are in column formation and about tree hundred yards away. I estimate grid D5"* –RumCake is letting Bigfoot know that they have an ambush opportunity approaching them, currently three hundred yards out around the field grid of D5.

*"I copy enemy squad approaching from the north in column formation, tree hundred yards, ETA?"* – Bigfoot wants to know how long he has to wake up his people and get them ready.

*"About five mikes."* –RumCake estimates five minutes. Bigfoot should realize that RumCake probably means two minutes.

*"I copy five mikes, thank you. Bigfoot out."* –Bigfoot has to get ready and is done jabbering on the radio.

*"RumCake out."* –RumCake is done as well.

## Enemy Sighting (Bad Example)

*"Yo Bigfoot "... "YO Bigfoot!"* – Can anybody hear me?

*"What!"*

*"You got tangos coming."* – Oh joy.

*"From where?"* – In front, behind, to the flanks, are they tunneling?

*"North of you"*

*"How many?"*

*"I dunno, maybe a squad. Hard to say for sure, but the guy in the back is a big fat guy who looks like he is having trouble keeping up. He should have stayed home with his bag of potato chips."*

*"Does he have a boonie hat on or a baseball cap?"* – And what does this have to do with an impending firefight?

*"Goony hat?"* – Who cares about a freakin hat?

*"No, BOONIE hat."*

*"Oh, yea, he's wearing a boonie hat."*

*"I know that guy, does he also have an M203?"*

*"Yea, looks like it. Friend of yours?"*

*"I owe him one. He shot me last game."*

*"Well, now's your chance."*

*"How far away is he?"*

*"About two hundred yards I think."*

*"Is he approaching from near the stream or that big tree?"*

*"What big tree?"*

*"The one that was hit by lighting."*

*"Oh. Near the stream then."*

Etc. . . . . .

Any professional listening would hope that one of the two would hurry up and freakin' die.

## Enemy Contact (Good Example)

*"ToeJam, ToeJam this is Armpit, come in."* – Armpit wants ToeJam to wake up and answer.

*"This is ToeJam go."* –Proceed with your transmission.

*"This is Armpit, we have enemy contact to our front near grid A7. Estimated two to three with light weapons. They were in defensive positions."* – A fireteam is slowing us down, just thought you should know in case that fireteam turns out to be a platoon and we get wiped out.

*"Copy that. Over run or break contact. Continue mission."* - ToeJam is saying thanks for the info, kill them quickly or go around them. I don't want you to get bogged down in a firefight when you have a mission to accomplish.

*"WilCo Toejam. Armpit out."* –Armpit has some mayhem to wreck.

*"ToeJam out."* – ToeJam is going to finish his lunch now.

## Enemy Contact (Bad Example)

*"We are getting shot at!"* – But not yet shot.

*"Who is 'we'?"* – Two mistakes one from caller and one from listener.

*"Uh… this is Armpit."*

*"Where are you?"*

*"Behind a tree where they can't see me."* – Gotta love Armpit, such a fount of information.

*"What tree?"*

*"A big one. They know I'm here and I can hear the BB's smacking against the tree. I think Bo-Bo got hit, but I can't see. At least one guy is shooting at me, maybe two. They can't move very well though because they have a large opening to the side and if they try to get through it I can shoot them pretty easily."* – of course Toejam can't tell Armpit to shut up and tell him what grid coordinates are.

*"What grid coordinate are you at?"*

*"I don't have a map"* – Armpit is a well-prepared noob who should be a rifleman instead of team leader.

*"How many are shooting at you?"* – ToeJam asks, realizing Armpit could be anywhere.

*"I don't know, at least one."* – One guy holding up a squad?

*"I meant how many enemy is your squad facing".*

*"How can I tell?"*

*"Guess."*

*"Maybe three or four."*

*"What are they doing?"*

*"Shooting at us."* – And if ToeJam was there, someone else would be shooting at Armpit.

Etc. . . . . . hopefully Armpit will get wasted soon.

## 3.2.7. Radios, RTO Organization

RTO's (Radio Telegraph Operators) are usually dedicated to a certain role and mission.

For instance, a company commander may have several RTO's; one for speaking with his platoon commanders, one for speaking with higher headquarters, one for speaking with close air support assets, one for artillery, etc. Because of all the radio operators following higher ranking commanders around the field they are frequently called antenna farms.

It is possible for a single person to carry multiple radios and monitor multiple frequencies, but a person can only talk on a single radio at a time. Trying to keep track of conversations on multiple radios becomes very difficult, if not impossible, when the adrenaline starts pumping and rounds are flying. Also, channel hopping can cause the RTO to miss callers, or when the RTO is talking on one channel they may miss something on another channel. In airsoft, the unit leaders are frequently their own RTO's so they can talk directly with their leaders.

There are three ways of using RTO's in most cases. In situation 1, the RTO is used to communicate with higher headquarters while the leader's radio is used to talk with subordinate units. In situation 2, the leader's radio is used to talk with his commander while the RTO communicates with subordinates. In Situation #3, the leader does not have a personal radio and communicates through his RTO's.

### 3.2.8. Practice

Radio communications should be practiced so that people get familiar with giving and receiving instructions and descriptions over the radio. This is a skill that must be developed. One method is for people to get radios, dress in civilian clothes and move each other around a park or area. For instance, a CO might direct elements to certain vantage points and have them describe what they see (number of windows, placement of windows, etc).

As lame as it may sound, radio communications should be practiced like regular battle drills to establish 'muscle memory' or in this case, a good habit. When the adrenaline hits it is always easier to go with habit than to think.

### 3.2.9. Radio Frequencies

Some people get more powerful and customizable radios (Motorola GP68's for instance). You have to program the frequencies and may need an FCC license to operate it, however. Here is a list of standard frequencies used by most family type radios to help you program your radio.

1. 462.5625
2. 462.5875
3. 462.6125
4. 462.6375
5. 462.6625
6. 462.6875
7. 462.7125
8. 467.5625
9. 467.5875
10. 467.6125
11. 467.6375

12. 467.6625
13. 467.6875
14. 467.7125

# 4. Hand Arm Signal Communications

Hand arm signals are excellent for communicating over distances where yelling won't work, you don't have a radio, in noisy environments or when talking could be dangerous and give away your position.

The disadvantage of hand arm signals is that you have to make yourself visible and you may need a little room to move. The person you want to communicate with also has to see you and can't be looking in a different direction. Squished into a creek bed while plastic doom flies overhead can make it kind of difficult to tell the squad to deploy online. In this case you should just yell because people aren't going to be looking at you anyway.

Hand arm signals are also very useful for Fireteams since most members don't always have radios or radios that work. There may be times that people have to work together and are not on the same frequency as well.

When you are crouched down behind a tree getting ready to engage the enemy it really helps to be able to communicate special instructions, numbers, location and activity of the enemy to other team members that may not see the bad guys. Other members of the squad should repeat the hand arm signal because not everyone can see (or will be watching) the squad/team leader. If everyone repeats the signal then a commander can effectively command a large number of people to accomplish a task without seeing everyone, having to shout or run around. Generally having all members of a squad repeat a hand arm signal requires discipline and/or training.

Military hand arm signals are designed to be visible at longer ranges. There are lots of places online and offline that show all the different hand arm signals. It is always interesting to note that rarely do these pictures of hand arm signals show people with rifles and wearing full gear. One interesting hand arm signal for "enemy sighted" can be confusing. Basically, it shows someone pointing their rifle in the direction of the enemy. So, what if someone is covering their fields of fire or waiting for an enemy to pop-out of a potential hide? When advancing on an enemy position how is the weapon being held? Some of them just don't make sense and can be pretty confusing.

Again, 'The Book' provides a good starting point. In airsoft and in real combat the hand arm signals shown in books are not always practical or usable. For instance, if a team is quietly approaching an enemy position, it isn't always practical for the team or squad leader to stand up where everyone can see him (like the enemy) and give the signal to deploy online. Very difficult to do while crouching behind a tree and holding a five-pound rifle. Usually it will be just a small team that has enough separation so that regular speech will work, but that won't help them to maintain stealth.

Keep in mind though, it is usually a bad move to stop aiming your weapon in the direction of the enemy who might look in your direction any second just so you can properly convey a hand arm signal.

HAND signals become much more useful in close quarters between team members. They are useful indoors as well as outdoors. Generally, there should be a format; number, action, distance - followed by a reaction. Here are some examples of hand arm signals. Squads and teams should establish their own SOP (Standard Operating Procedures). Find out what works for you.

## 4.1. Hand Arm Signals

### 4.1.1. Assemble

**Pointing at the sky and making a circle.** This is used to get everyone to assemble close to you so they can hear you speak. While this is not tactically advisable (because it makes a nice target for automatic fire or grenades), sometimes you just have to get people together.

When combined with another hand/arm signal (APL, SAW, etc), it is a request for those individuals to come up. For instance, using the SAW hand/arm signal and then the Assemble means that SAW gunners should move up and rally around the leader.

### 4.1.2. Rally Point

**Pointing at the ground or notable terrain feature and making a circle.** This hand/arm signal is used to designate a spot where the unit should assemble in the event that they get separated, killed, or have to retreat under fire. Rally points should be something easily recognizable; they should also be able to provide defensive positions for people while they wait for others to arrive.

Rally points are extremely useful on larger fields and help keep effective squads and teams together.

### 4.1.3. Halt

**Hand up and open**. This just means hold up for a minute (or more) while something is taken care of; either a scout is sent forward, intelligence information is relayed or to take a break. Once the signal is received and passed back, team members may take a knee, maybe take cover, and/or face away from the center of the formation. In a single file, every other person should face in the opposite direction (left or right) of the person in front of him. Team members should also evaluate surrounding cover and concealment for use in the event enemy contact is made. Team members should not get too comfortable as this is likely to be temporary. In the event it will take longer, the command to take a knee (or take cover) should be given.

### 4.1.4. Freeze

**Holding up a fist.** This means FREEZE, do not move, do not breath loud, do not take your weapon off safe, remain absolutely still and do not make a noise, do not ask questions, do not pass go. It means FREEZE - as in completely motionless and silent. Team members should immediately begin assessing the local area for potential cover and concealment locations and anticipate a firefight at any second. Movement can make noise or attract attention. DON'T!

### 4.1.5. Patrol Leader Up

**Shake the collar tab of your uniform** (to signify rank). This means the leader, patrol leader, senior team member, etc, should come forward because there is something ahead that needs attention. Either the pointman has a question, has found something or is lost. After passing on the signal everyone should take a knee and face outboard unless the formation is still moving.

## 4.1.6. Assistant Patrol Leader Up (Assistant Patrol Leader or Team Leader's)

**Clapping the shoulder patch of the uniform.** This is the signal for the assistant patrol leader(s) to come forward. In most cases, special instructions will be given to deploy a team or assistance is needed. After passing on the signal everyone should take a knee and face outboard unless the formation is still moving.

### 4.1.7. SAW Gunner Up

**Using a pumping motion with the non-shooting arm, palm up**. This is the sign for "SAW gunner" to advance, in most cases so that the team/patrol leader can position him in a good spot or where they may need the suppressing fire.

### 4.1.8. Hasty Ambush

**This is a fist punching motion in the direction the ambush should occur.** After passing on the hand arm signal, team members should get in a line facing the direction in which the fist was punched and get ready for combat and find cover and concealment as quickly and quietly as possible. Think, "We are going to hit them, hard."

## 4.1.9. Enemy Sighted

**This hand/arm signal is basically pointing your weapon in the direction of the enemy.** Personally, I don't care for this one because it is too easy to ignore or otherwise disregard. People are ALWAYS pointing their weapons in different directions; it is called covering your sector. It can be exaggerated however. I prefer the "Enemy" hand signal and then pointing in the direction.

### 4.1.10. Get down/Take a Knee

**With the hand open, palm down patting toward the ground.** This means take a knee. You are likely to be in the area for a few minutes. It is also a good idea to evaluate the local cover and concealment, moving to get behind something more protective if possible. In some cases, this may also mean take cover so people should be ready for the firefight to begin at a moment's notice.

### 4.1.11. Take cover

**With the hand vertical and open, a downward sweep is made so the open palm is facing down and then moved from left to right.** This tells people to get down and take cover. After passing on the signal team members should get down and take cover, preparing for an imminent firefight.

### 4.1.12. Danger Area

**Slashing the throat with an open knife hand.**
This is used to indicate a danger area ahead.
Danger areas are places where contact is likely.
It can be a trail, a clearing, hill top, or some other
feature where the enemy has good observation
and the unit is unlikely to see the enemy until the
shooting starts. This is an indication that people
should be more careful and ready to act more
quickly.

## 4.1.13. Slow Down

**Palm flat to the ground and the hand/arm moving slowly left and right.** This is used to tell people to slow down the pace or decrease the rate of fire.

## 4.1.14. Speed Up

**Fist pointed up with a pumping motion.** This means pick up the pace or fire faster. It also means to double time or run.

## 4.1.15. Change Direction

**A knife hand jabbing in the new direction of travel.** This indicates which way someone should go.

## 4.1.16. Range/Numbers

Holding up fingers to indicate a number. If there are more than five, then holding down the various fingers indicates the number. To change a number (such as 25, would be "two, fist, five"). This is how you indicate the range or number (of enemies). Two hundred would be a "two, fist, zero, fist, zero."

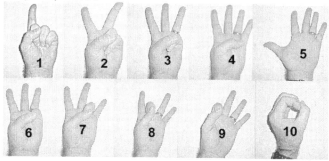

### 4.1.17. Ready?

**Thumbs up OR holding an open palm toward the person you are talking to. They should respond with the same signal if they are ready.** This is the official hand arm signal. Personally, I prefer the thumbs up. However, this is easier to see at longer ranges.

## 4.1.18. Shift Left (or Right)

**Using an open palm to 'push' them in the direction you want them to go**. This is a suggestion to move in another direction in order to spread out more or to get properly placed.

### 4.1.19. Spread Out/Disperse

**With the back of the hand to the center of the chest pushing out with the open hand.** This is a strong recommendation to spread out. Spreading out is good because this makes it harder for a burst of automatic fire to get you all. It also makes you harder to see and makes it harder for a grenade to take you all out. The 'book' usually shows a person using two hands. Personally, I think if you take both hands off your weapon you are begging to be SHOT.

## 4.1.20. Close it up

**Open hand, palm pushing toward the center of the chest. (If there were two hands they would be clapping.)** This is the opposite of Spread Out/Disperse and means people should close the distance. The 'book' usually shows a person using two hands. Again, personally, I think if you take both hands off your weapon you are begging to be SHOT.

## 4.1.21. Cease Fire

**Waving the knife hand in front of the face.**
This is an indication to cease fire.

**The forearm is angled across the chest pointing at the opposite shoulder.** This is the signal for Fireteam. It may be preceded by a number of fingers held up, like one, two or three. This indicates WHICH Fireteam. In most cases it will be something like, "1", "Fireteam", "Assemble" or "Flank" which means that first Fireteam should move up to the leader for orders or deployment instructions. This may also be used by the team leader to inform his team he is about to give them an order such as a formation change.

## 4.1.23. Squad

**The hand is held out at arm's length and only the hand is waved.** It looks gay and signifies Squad. In most cases it will be followed by additional commands, like a number, formation, assemble, etc. Personally, I think they did this to help new boot lieutenants look gay. Just sayin'. ☺

## 4.2. Formations

### 4.2.1. Column Formation

**A big circle with the entire arm straight and pointing in the direction the column should be moving.** Single file or double column depending on the terrain. This is the fastest form of movement for a group from one location to another. Tactically, though, it is not advisable.

## 4.2.2. Wedge

**A pyramid is made by pointing both arms down to the side at a forty five degree angle.** This can apply to the squad or Fireteam. The wedge is best used for fast movement where the enemy's location is not known. It allows for the team (or squad) to rapidly deploy, face the enemy in a line and focus firepower to the front and half the firepower to either side. This reduces the team (or squad's) vulnerability to flank attacks. When the enemy's exact location is known, the line or skirmish line should be used.

### 4.2.3. Echeleon Left

**The arms are held out at a forty-five degree angle - left arm is high, right arm low.** The Echeleon is a formation that focuses combat firepower to the front and to the left. It is vulnerable to fire from the right front. It reduces the vulnerability of flanking from the left. This is not a highly used formation in most airsoft or paintball games.

## 4.2.4. Echeleon Right

**The arms are held out at a forty-five degree angle - right arm is high, left arm low.** The Echeleon is a formation that focuses combat firepower to the front and to the right. It is vulnerable to fire from the left front. It reduces the vulnerability of flanking from the right. This is not a highly used formation in most airsoft or paintball games.

### 4.2.5.  On Line/Skirmish Line

**Both arms held out to either side like an airplane.** This is the optimum combat formation for attack.  It focuses all firepower to the front, but is vulnerable to flank attacks.  Team members on either side of the formation should take care to watch for the enemy flank attacks. This does not require the formation be perfectly on line, depending on the terrain.  The goal of this formation is that everyone can fire forward without endangering someone to either side.

### 4.2.6. V Formation

**Pointing both arms up at the sky at forty-five degree angles.** This is primarily a squad type formation. It is very difficult to control and has limited use. It is like a reverse wedge in that it focuses combat firepower and the ability to rapidly deploy to a rear attack. This is more commonly used during a retreat or when guarding the rear of a larger formation. This is highly unlikely to be used in an airsoft or paintball game.

## 4.3. Hand Signals

These are generally not something you find in most books, pictures, forums, or guides.

### 4.3.1. Enemy

**Placing the open hand over the face to simulate a mask.** Bad guys wear masks. This is usually followed by other hand arm signals, such as a direction. A third command is usually then given like hasty ambush, take cover, get on line, etc.

## 4.3.2. Walking

**Two fingers, pointing down and moving.**
Looks like legs walking. This is usually
preceded by a signal of WHO is walking (like the
enemy, or friendlies) and a direction.

### 4.3.3. Friendlies

**Thumbs up.** This is a very versatile and common gesture that has many uses. It means okay, friendlies, no worries, etc. In this case, usually a direction is identified followed by the thumbs up. This means don't shoot what comes from that direction. Don't forget to tell the people approaching from that direction that you are friendly! Passing this on indicates understanding.

### 4.3.4. **Okay?**

**Thumbs up.** Like the friendly signal the proper use of this is not preceded by a direction or any other information, except maybe "You!" Just thumbs up at the person. The correct response is a thumb up.

## 4.3.5. You

**Pointing directly at the person.** This means YOU and is usually followed by additional commands - go there, look there, etc.

### 4.3.6. Go there

**A closed fist thumping the forehead, like grabbing a unicorn horn and then pointing at a location.** This means the person should go to that location. It may be followed by a 'look' signal as well. A relevant example would be to tell someone to go to a certain location and cover a certain direction.

**Two fingers pointed at the eyes and then in a certain direction.** This means look there. In this case looking is the same as covering. You should look with your eyes AND your weapon. Additionally, pointing to your ears means listening.

## 4.3.8. **Silence**

**Holding a finger to the lips.** Kind of no brainer - it means SHUT UP, close your pie-hole, stop making noise and be "vewy, vewy" quiet!

**Using the entire shoulder and then pointing in a certain direction.** This means move out and be ready for anything.

## 4.3.10. Flank

**The hand is cupped and a cutting motion is used and then pointed in the direction the flankers should go**. The flanking team should move out and prepare to envelope the enemy.

**With only the middle finger extended it is pointed down at something.** This means I'm in a bad situation and need some covering fire while I get out of this unpleasant mess. Help is needed. Please note, do NOT use this hand signal unless the person you are using it with understands what it means AND in a simulated combat condition. I would not condone using this hand signal at any other time. It ain't nice and might lead to friendly fire.

### 4.3.12. Too bad, so sad, I'm covered

**Only the middle finger of a hand is extended at the sky or some object.** This means, sorry buddy, would like to help, but I can't. Please note, do NOT use this hand signal unless the person you are using it with understands what it means AND in a simulated combat condition. I would not condone using this hand signal at any other time. It ain't nice and might lead to some friendly fire.

# 5.   Voice Communication

Nothing can be more effective than walking up to someone and telling them something. The listener can see hand motions, facial gestures and can easily pick up nuances. During a face to face conversation, more information is traded than just words.

When talking DO NOT WHISPER. This is NOT quieter than talking. You should talk in a very low and soft voice; exhale first if you can as that will reduce the hissing noises. The "ssss" of speech (predominant in whispering) carries farther than most people know. A low voice is much stealthier.

Being close enough to talk is a big advantage, but it can also be a disadvantage. First off, the enemy can sometimes hear you; the enemy speaks the same language as you and is very likely to understand what you want to do. If they know what you plan to do, then they can more easily oppose you. Also, when you are close and talking with someone, your attention may not always be on your surroundings and the closer you are, the juicier the target you become.

For instance, when you yell out that you are throwing a grenade, the enemy knows to expect one (and considering some of the players I've seen, the enemy will likely pick it up and throw it back!) If you tell your buddies to cover you while you do something, then you can bet your bottom dollar that the enemy will seek to discourage this and make it harder for your buddies to do their job. Radio communications can also be intercepted and overheard. However, you look at it, there is a chance (although frequently small) that the enemy might hear you speaking to your team mates and since everyone is pretty much speaking the same language, you can bet they will understand and work to crush your plans beneath a hail of plastic doom.

Here are a couple of things to consider; on average, the enemy is not going to hear you unless they are pretty close or you are yelling. This is NOT the case in CQB, aka, close quarters battle. The enemy might be right around the corner, just behind the window, under the stairs, or in the closet. In wooded areas the chance of the enemy hearing you are actually pretty low unless you are yelling (like telling your buddy to cover you).

The best methods of confusing the enemy and preventing the Opfor from listening, understanding and then thwarting your plans is to use code words. Using code words takes constant practice. They should be short and very easy to remember. You should always include your call sign when yelling a code word or action. This lets your friends know exactly who is doing what as they might not always recognize your voice. Friendlies should repeat your words as well. It also tells the enemy, if they are listening, who is about to clobber them.

Here are some examples;

**"<Your callsign> yellow!"** could tell everyone in range that you are out of ammo and cannot fire for a short time.

**"<Your call sign> Green!"** lets them know you are ready, advancing, have heard the command, have reloaded, etc.

**"<Your call sign> Red!"** lets everyone know that you are having a weapon malfunction, are reloading magazines or something like that. For whatever reason, you will be out of the fight for a little bit.

**"<Your call sign> Brown!"** could mean that you are stuck behind cover and can't move, or you need to change your undies.

**"<Your call sign> White!"** could mean that you don't have any cover and are in a bad situation.

**"<Your call sign> Loki."** could mean you are trying to flank left (Loki starts with an "L" for "Left") and may be easier to remember.

**"<Your Call Sign> Romeo."** means flanking right (Romeo starts with an "R" for "Right"). It could also mean you are about to get intimate with the enemy.

**"<Your call sign> Pineapple left window."** means you are throwing a grenade (or shooting) into the left window.

**"Oh, shit! Grenade! Ahhhh!"** means that someone just threw a grenade at you. The "Oh shit!" and "Ahhhh!" part is optional, of course. Generally, you shouldn't swear on the airsoft field, but in some instances, it might slip out. It always gives me a warm fuzzy when I hear the enemy say that. You should swear like that too if you want to give your enemy a warm fuzzy happy feeling.

You should be starting to get the idea. ***Remember, keep it simple*** because when the rounds fly you don't want to be standing there thinking "does pineapple mean enter the room or a grenade is outbound?"

Team and squad members should also repeat the commands when possible (hence the use of the call sign and status). If the squad leader yells out "Squad On line" then everyone should repeat it because not everyone will have heard the squad leader. With commands, "On line" or "Wedge", etc. repeating it also helps to designate a center point for people to focus on. "Does he mean get on line with him or Fluffy Bunny?" can lead to people going everywhere. Using the call sign also indicates an order as well.

Properly said it would be, "Squad on line with Tinkerbell." Everyone would repeat it and look for Tinkerbell to get on line with him in the direction that he is facing. He would then become the orientation for the formation.

## 5.1. Talking at Night

Hand arm signals don't work well in the dark and voices carry very well, along with any kind of noise. See **The Airsoft Bible: Book of Darkness** for more detail on night ops. One thing to remember is that whispering is NOT quieter than talking. The hissing noise carries much further than a low soft voice. When talking at night, make sure that you exhale and then talk in a low voice.  It will be quieter and more understandable.

## 5.2. Challenge/Password

Night is a good example of when a challenge/password is most effective.  However, there may be times during day games where a challenge/password is useful, like when the teams are 'mixed up' and identifying friend from foe is a challenge (where green is mixed with tan for instance).

When in a fixed position, only one person should give the challenge and that person should be behind something solid.  Other players should be nearby and ready to fire, keeping their position and presence a secret until it is time to unleash.  Be aware that the enemy might decide to start firing the second they hear the challenge and they will have a good idea where the voice is coming from.

There are several ways of using a challenge/password:

### 5.2.1. Common

Using the common challenge and password method, two words are selected.  For instance, "Diamond" and "Blue".  The Challenger calls out "Diamond" and then the person(s) being challenged must say "Blue" or they get lit up.  Short and simple.  Also, easy to decipher.  I recall one game where we discovered the enemy challenge password very early in the scenario and used it to inflict heavy casualties on the enemy. Later on, in the game the enemy got smart. One conversation;

"Diamond!" - Enemy
"Blue!" - Friendly
"That's not it!" - Enemy
"Red! Green! Yellow!" - Friendly. Pop, pop, pop!

Suffice it to say the enemy, had changed it.

Anyone with half a brain and a set of ears can usually figure it out very quickly.

## 5.2.2. Encrypted

This is more effective, but a little more complicated. It isn't perfect, but it is better than the common method. Like the common method, the challenge/password consists of two words. For instance, "Baseball" and "Cake". The challenger makes up a sentence using the challenge word, for instance "Who won the baseball world series in nineteen sixty-eight?" The person being challenged must come up with a sentence using the word "Cake" for instance, "That's a piece of cake. It was the New York Yankees!"

If the enemy was nearby and listening they might approach the sentry and respond to the challenge with just "New York Yankees!" in which case they are greeted with a hail of automatic fire. Doesn't matter that the Yankees didn't play in the '68 World Series, which some baseball genius might realize, but that is beside the point.

### 5.2.3. Numerical

This is trickier and requires some math skills. The password is a single number. For instance - eight. The person challenging calls out "Three!" the person being challenged replies with a number that adds up to the password and replies "Five!" The challenger should change it up each time. Of course, it might be fun to also use the common method on occasion, but that would be too easy.

### 5.2.4. Numerical Encrypted

The same as numerical except 'encrypted' in a regular phrase. If the password were nine, the challenger would say "Four red cupcakes" and the person being challenged would say "I've got five blue ones." This makes it harder to guess what is going on, but not exactly impossible.

### 5.2.5. Running Password

The running password is only used in extreme situations, like you are being chased back into friendly lines. It is easily translated as "Please, pretty please, don't shoot me I'm on your side and I don't wanna get shot because I'm running at you!" When there is time, the standard challenge password routine should be used but in emergencies the running password works. The person(s) that SHOULD be challenged is usually running (hence the name "running" password) and is usually yelling it out. Anybody not yelling it out gets SHOT.

## 5.3. Codewords

Considering that the enemy speaks the same language as you do and you can't REALLY kill them, it is likely that they will overhear your conversations, as they sit there dead, waiting for respawn or lurking around the corner waiting for you to peek. Sometimes, this means that the enemy can gain valuable intelligence on what you plan to do, where you plan to go, where you are deployed and who is doing it. As soon as they can pass on that info, you will find a nasty surprise waiting for you.

Enter code words. Usually very simple names for common places or people, they can cause uncertainty and confusion to the enemy. They can also cause confusion to friendlies! For instance, referring to HQ as "Happy Queen" will make the enemy wonder what you are talking about. Someone who wasn't awake at the briefing will start watching behind themselves and other players more often.

That said, you should use as few as possible and keep them as SIMPLE as possible. In most cases (specifically open plays), you shouldn't use them at all because they will just confuse people. I've noticed people don't listen very well at open plays. MilSim events usually attract a slightly higher caliber of player and there tends to be more planning that goes into good MilSim events.

One trick to using code words (and a way that helps people remember them) is to use the first character and change the rest. For instance, "Headquarters" becomes "Happy

Queen", "Gold City" become "Grimy Cow", etc. It becomes a fifty-fifty sometimes. If you make it too complicated everyone forgets and doesn't use it anyway; if it is too simple the enemy might figure it out.

# 6. Other Communication Methods

Radios, hand arm signals and yelling are not the only methods of command and control. The Chinese use whistles and during the civil war both sides used bugles, flares and weapons fire to communicate as well.

When my brother and I were younger, we used wolf howls to communicate because a howl can be heard and understood much further away than shouting. On the airsoft field this can freak people out, especially when they realize a conversation is occurring and that they have no clue what it is about. It was very simple. One howl – "come here" or "I am here"; two howls – "where are you?"; three howls – "I'm coming."

The key to communication is COMMUNICATION. Everyone must know and understand the methods being used. Everyone should practice them and review them frequently. Radios are great, but when there are hundreds of players on the field there is a very limited number of useable radio channels so squads will be 'stepping' on each other or jamming each other's communications constantly. This makes alternate forms of communication crucial to successful operations. Hand arm signals are great, if you are in the open and can see everyone and everyone is watching you. Yelling isn't real effective once the plastic begins to fly in large fights because EVERYONE is yelling about one thing or another, nobody is watching you, except the enemy, and people are stressed.

You can also rest assured that when you desperately need your radios to work, they won't. Either the battery has died, the channel got changed, your radio fell out of its holster, the headset got unplugged, the radio got turned down too far, you are on the wrong encryption channel, your headset is broken, etc. There are MANY things that can go wrong and chances are you will experience ALL of them at different times and when it is least convenient.

This is one reason the fatality rate of squad leaders and platoon commanders is so high in real world combat. These combat leaders are running around the battle field trying to communicate with and command their troops, see what the enemy is doing and find out what higher command wants them to do about the situation. Running around makes you a target. Targets get shot.

When using alternative means of communication, they must remain *simple*. A few of the best commands are: attack, retreat, and assemble. The more complex you make it the more you increase the chance of confusion and error. Short simple commands are more successful than complex ones. They should be distinctive and clear. Veterans who work together a lot will have an entire language of their own.

A whistle is an excellent tool for communication. It is very distinct and loud, not heavily used and can be heard by people without special equipment (like a radio). Using a combination of short blasts and long blasts provide instructions to a squad or platoon. Think Morse code.

I've seen amateurs go hog wild with the idea of code words and call signs, then when the fecal matter hits the spinning blades, nobody can remember anything and chaos and confusion rule the day. ALWAYS keep it simple and easy! Make sure it is written down when possible to help remember and practice, practice, practice. And don't forget to PRACTICE.

In World War 2 during the invasion of Europe, paratroopers used simple clicking cricket clackers. If you weren't familiar with them they sounded like crickets, but only friendly troops had them and were familiar with their use. They saved a lot of lives at night because friendly troops were able to identify each other quickly.

The key is imagination and training.

# 7. Comm Plans and Organization

If radios will be used, then there should be a comm plan. In most cases event organizers will say "Event organizers and emergencies are on channel 1, Tan forces use odd numbers, Green forces use even numbers" and then let the players pick a channel from there. The organizer might also ask that the team captains be on a certain channel so they can communicate with them.

That is a simple comm plan. A more detailed comm plan assigns radio channels, call signs and code words. KEEP IT SIMPLE! If possible, write it down beforehand and make sure everyone has a copy, especially squad, team and element leaders.

## 7.1. Organization

When a squad is working with a larger unit (like a platoon or even just a team) and they are operating on their own radio channel, then they should designate someone to monitor the separate command channel. This RTO can be extremely useful in reporting the squad's current situation, location, etc to higher command without interfering with the Squad Leader and what he is doing. Some people may recommend that the squad leader operate on the command channel, but that means he is not commanding his squad, he is just listening for orders and a good squad leader is going to spend more time talking with his people than to the commander. Additionally it might be useful for the squad leader to have a second radio specifically for talking with command. The problem with this is that the squad leader can get hammered with information overload; commanding a squad, evaluating the situation and enemy, and also listening to command can all cause problems which can lead to bad decisions or missed communications.

Team leaders should have radios and should talk directly with the squad leader. Team members may have radios as well, but should limit their radio traffic when possible. Key elements in a team should also have radios (point man, scouts, snipers, etc). Too many team leaders and team members trying to talk on a channel can bring a squad's communication to a grinding halt. Some squads operate well when everyone has a radio, but just be aware, it is possible to overload everyone with too much info and traffic.

The same thing applies to platoon commanders/leaders. Having a dedicated RTO to talk to and work with higher command is a major advantage and lets the platoon commander concentrate on leading the platoon.

## 7.2. Comm Plan

Unit leaders at all levels should have a communication plan, hopefully the same one. When possible, it should be memorized, in general it should be written down by everyone with a radio. Not all items will be required depending on the game and resources. A good comm plan has the following pieces of information:

- o Call Signs and channels for leaders, XO's and VIP's
- o Call Signs and channels for medics/Corpsmen
- o Call signs and channels for units
- o Code words for possible objectives or locations.
- o Challenge Passwords
- o Running Password
- o Primary location of leaders, Medics/Corpsmen, VIP's, etc.
- o Rally Points
- o Any special communication gear and how it is to be used (whistles, chem lights, colored flash lights, flares, etc)

# 8.    Equipment

## 8.1. Overview

Everyone thinks 'radio' when they think of communications. Accessories are an afterthought to most amateurs and some professionals. Electronic stores, sports stores and large department stores usually carry radios of one kind or another. Getting a radio is a good start. It is highly recommended that after a weapon, you invest in a radio. Shortly after getting your radio, though, you will realize how bothersome it can be to keep clipping and unclipping it from your gear to talk with people, assuming you haven't lost it. Then there is the hard lesson learned when you are busy talking on the radio and you get shot by a bad guy that you didn't know was there, but who had no problem finding you and your loud radio.

Yep. Having a radio is awesome. What is even more awesome (and cool looking) is a good headset; be it a boom mic, a throat mic or some variant thereof. It is even better when that headset actually works! Then you need some way to keep your radio safe and secure.

## 8.2. Choosing a Radio

There are many cheap radios and you will get what you pay for. Even though a radio may say "Range is 26 miles" what they really mean is that if you are on a mountain top and can actually SEE the other person who is 25.9 miles away, you might actually be able to talk with them. If there is anything else between you (like trees, leaves, bushes, air, etc.) then the range will drop dramatically, sometimes to 2 feet. Sunspot activity, antenna, weak batteries, the alignment of the moons around Jupiter, etc. can all affect the quality of your radio communications. Do not expect to be able to talk to someone a half mile away despite the fact that you have a "26 mile range" radio.

Most, if not all, radios have multiple channels. Some of them have 'sub channels' or privacy channels. These channels are generally the same on all radios that are available to civilians. In most cases it doesn't matter the brand of radio, channel 1 (usually for event organizers) is still channel 1. This is good and bad. Good because you should be able to speak with everyone on that channel, bad because if there are a lot of people, the channels can become congested. Very bad if you are sharing that channel with the people who you are shooting at.

Privacy or sub channels are good and help segregate traffic, but can be overridden by someone who is on the same channel and has a stronger broadcast. For example, if you are on Channel 4, subchannel 3, then anyone on Channel 4 (or any other subchannel) can broadcast over you and interfere with your traffic.

One thing to keep in mind is that while FRS (Family Radio Service) radios may all have the same channels, there are some differences in transmission strength, privacy channels, broadcast quality, etc. Transmitting from one radio to another of the same type may be fine, but transmitting to a radio of a different type/brand may garble your communication and you might not be as easily understood because the volume may need to be adjusted, etc.

## 8.2.1. FRS

Most radios available for purchase are FRS (Family Radio Service.) There are only a select number of channels available and they are limited in power and range. They are cheap and common. In most cases they are sufficient for most games and this is what you will see the most.

## 8.2.2. GMRS

Then there are the GMRS (General Mobile Radio Service) radios which require an FCC license to operate. The GMRS radios can broadcast at a higher power, increasing range and they also have a much wider range of channels. Some of them can be programmed and they all have the price tag to match their features. A lot of the more established teams prefer to use GMRS for a couple reasons. They are more powerful, meaning better range and reception. They also have more channels available, which can be critical at large games

with hundreds of players. The big disadvantage
of the GMRS is that you must have a license to
operate them (mostly it is just paying the license
fee, nothing special).

## 8.3. Choosing a Headset

It is always recommended that you get a
headset. Be it a throat mic, a boom mic, an ear
piece, etc. If you don't, then you have to fumble
with the radio, taking it on and off your gear
when you want to listen or transmit (unless you
attach it to your shoulder harness). Additionally,
it is bad form to be sneaking up on someone and
then have to scramble for the volume when
somebody starts asking who's winning the local
football game, thereby deafening you and more
importantly advertising your presence and giving
you a quick (hopefully) introduction to the
Opfor's automatic weapon.

There are many different types of
headsets. You ALWAYS want one that is easy
to reach and has "PTT" or Push-To-Talk
operations. "VOX" is Voice Operated
Xmitter(transmitting). It means when you talk,
your radio transmits, no button pushing required.
*Do not use VOX on pain of death.* Nobody will
like you if you do. VOX might seem cool, but it
never works that way when the fecal matter hits
the spinning air motion device. If you breathe
hard, moan, fire your weapon, etc. you will start
transmitting and either miss important
information or prevent other people from
receiving or sending important information.

Always mount the PTT button in a place you can quickly access it without having to look and where it won't snag on vegetation, your weapon OR accidently get pressed. Make sure the headset is secure and won't fall off when you run and crawl. Taping the wires to your gear with subdued black electrician's tape is generally a good idea.

Another important factor when getting a headset is the people listening to you. Some headsets make the sender sound like they have a box of rocks in their mouth and this simply is not a good thing. Make sure to test the quality of your transmissions with the people you will be speaking with the most. Personally, I prefer a PTT button on a separate wire that I run down my arm where I then Velcro it to a finger. This way I can push the button between two fingers or between a finger and the weapon without removing my hand from my weapon.

There are several things to consider when getting a headset. The most important thing is that it must work, kind of a no-brainer, but it is interesting to note that many people buy a headset THINKING it will work when it doesn't. It should also be comfortable and easy to use.

Most radios take a headset or other attachment. Some may take earphones, some take external handsets, some take full blown headsets. There are several different types of pins. There are at least four different types of pins, in two and single connector. For instance, there are two types of Motorola two-pin adapters. They may or may not work in other Motorola or brands of radios.

My suggestion? Check online and make sure that they list your radio as compatible. Good luck with that too. One site that I use a lot is www.kawamall.com. They have adapters for almost every system that you can imagine and they list what they are compatible with. Prices are excellent as well, but just remember, you get what you pay for.

Everyone has different preferences and body types. What works for one person may not work for another. Personally, I prefer a throat mic and earbud with an extra PTT cable. Some people find a strap wrapped around their throat to be unpleasant and prefer to have a big plastic cup attached to the side of their ear by multiple straps that make them look like a hospital patient. The important thing is that it works for you. At a minimum, you should get an earbud so that any transmissions cannot be heard by the enemy which could be in a nearby bush, around the corner, etc.

Here are a couple of different headsets in use along with advantages and disadvantages.

It must be said again that you will get what you pay for.

### 8.3.1. **Throat Mic**

There are two types of throat mics. Essentially there are two pieces to a throat mic; the earpiece and the throat piece. The throat piece should be placed just to the side of the Adam's apple and the ear piece goes in an ear. The throat mic picks up the vibrations in your throat and converts that to voice. Usually this works great, BUT test it and have people tell you what you sound like. If they report crystal clear, try moving it around your throat. There are two basic types. One shaped like a big U and one that chokes you like a band. The U-shaped ones tend to move around more, especially if you run and crawl or are otherwise active. You may find it shifting and people won't be able to understand you. The choker, on the other hand, tends to be pretty stable but some people feel like they are being choked and don't like something wrapped around their neck.

**Throat mic choker, with extra PTT button and earbud.**

8.3.2. **Bone Mic**

This is another unique type of mic. Basically, there is only a single piece, the one that plugs into your ear. It uses the vibrations in the ear canal when you speak to convert that to a signal that it then transmits as voice. This is nice in that both the speaker AND the ear bud is one in the same. These are rarer and they don't work for everyone. The PTT button is usually in line between the earpiece and radio. The disadvantage is that you have to take your hands off your weapon and feel around for the PTT button. Usually there is a clip so that you can clip it somewhere you can get to it easily.

**Bone mic with extra cable PTT**

### 8.3.3. Ear Piece

This is basically an earpiece that you attach to your ear and the microphone is somewhere along the cable. A lot of cell phone headsets are like this. There might also be a PTT button on the microphone as well. The advantage of these is that there is only a single cable from ear to radio with a PTT button somewhere in line. The disadvantage is that you have to take your hands off of your weapon and feel around for the PTT button. Usually there is a clip so you can clip it somewhere you can get to it easily.

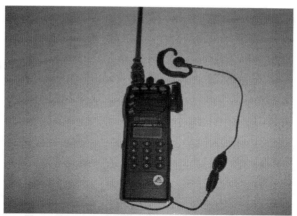

**Ear Piece with in line PTT button**

### 8.3.4. Hand Set

A worse-case-scenario type, but it can be useful if you carry more than a single radio. Such as what police use, this is a speaker/microphone at the end of a cable. Clipping it to your shoulder gear is the best use here. The problems are two-fold. You have to take your hand off your weapon to push-to-talk and when you receive a transmission everyone in the vicinity can hear it. Personally, I use this as a radio for event organizers or for my command channel. Keeping it turned off or down to a minimum most of the time. The advantage of this is that when carrying two radios you can still use one ear like normal instead of plugging in two headsets. It is a tradeoff.

**Handset**

### 8.3.5. Boom mic

There are several versions of the boom mic. For the most part, they consist of an ear piece, a piece of plastic that sticks out toward your mouth, and the PTT button, which is usually located somewhere between the ear piece and the radio. These are the most common and can be some of the most annoying. If the boom mic is too close, too far or improperly placed, you cannot understand the person transmitting. Some models cover the entire ear and are strapped to the head. Some just hook onto the ear. The, um, 'strap-ons' tend to be more rugged than the others, usually have larger PTT buttons and industrial strength clips. The little cheap ones that come with some radios have a nasty tendency to fall off when you start running and may not provide the best voice quality. The large PTT buttons make it quicker and easier to access than the smaller ones. Some are round and you almost have to stick your finger in them to activate. These are good because they are accidently pushed less often (like when lying down or prone).

**Headset with large PTT button**

**Inexpensive boom mic with in line PTT button**

## 8.4. Other Useful Accessories

**PTT button** – some of the better accessory kits have an extra-long PTT button. You can string this along your arm to your non-shooting hand and attach it in a way that is convenient for you. Done properly you can squeeze it between your finger and thumb or between your finger and weapon, etc, in order to transmit. I like the detachable kind so that I can take off my gear without having to unwire myself.

**Radio case** – This is a critical piece of equipment. It should give your radio some protection, keep it from getting lost, keep the wires from getting tangled, and of course hold your radio where you can get to it to change channels when some noob jams the channel with a hot mic.

**Electrician's tape** – This is really good to have in order to secure the wires of your radio so they are not snagging on everything around you. Do not use brightly colored or glossy electrician's tape. Go for the subdued, black tape when possible. Make sure that you have enough play in the wires for a full range of body movement. Remember that when you are crawling through thick vegetation, if the wires are not secured they are likely to snag and get pulled out or damaged.

## 8.5. Extra Batteries

Kind of a no brainer. It is guaranteed that your radio battery will start to die when you need it the most. Radios are designed that way, I'm sure.

## 8.6. Placement and Wearing

Protect your gear from hits. It seems normal to place the radio display panel facing out for you and others to see. Those display panels crack when hit by high velocity plastic. Turn it around to face your body and let the OpFor shoot at the back side. It is a lot less likely to do any damage.

## 8.7. VOX

Turn it off, disable it, do NOT use it. I have *never* seen it work properly. VOX is activated by sound. It usually takes a second to activate as well and you don't always know it has activated. So, IF it transmits, the person listening may only get part of the message. This also means that when you are talking and you think you are transmitting, you are not. When you don't think you are transmitting, you are. And when you are breathing hard, everyone can hear how out of shape you are and when you shoot your weapon you might get some less than friendly fire in the way of encouragement to stop jamming the airwaves.

## About the Author

Since he was knee high to a grass hopper he played "guns". In

that day and age when he was a kid they just made noise and didn't fire projectiles or anything. William Frisbee recalls staying out late at night with a bunch of friends, worried more about getting spotted and 'killed' than about rattlesnakes, water moccasins or big rabid elephant eating spiders back in the 70's. In retrospect, it is a surprise he survived his early years. Since the earliest age, he had planned on joining the Army; his mother was Army, uncles and cousins Army. So naturally, when it came time, he joined the US Marines and he has never come to regret that decision. He wanted to be infantry and that is exactly what he was.

William Frisbee started playing paintball in 1989 after having been in the Marines for a year. Being a big tough Marine (and also a boot), with quality combat training, it was a humbling experience to say the least. He was barely able to hold his own against two civilians who knew the field and weapons much better than he did and the first casualty was arrogance. He has been playing off and on ever since. William started playing 'airsoft' in 1990 with gas powered MP5's in the barracks (the FPS was like 3). When he got out of the Marines in 1992, he was a Corporal and the last billet held was infantry Squad Leader. A veteran of Desert Storm, he came in #2 in the Hawaii Infantry Squad Leader school (about 40 other NCO's), and 2nd in Terrorist Counteraction in Okinawa. During his time with 1st Battalion, 3rd Marines he was a SAW Gunner on Competition Squad, an elite squad taken from the best volunteers of a company that competed at the Battalion, Regimental and then Division level. The squad came in 2nd place at the Division competition in Okinawa. William has always had an interest in small unit tactics and infantry techniques and it has continued to this day.

These days he can be found playing airsoft, going to the gym, writing, reading, spending time with his family or tinkering with computers.

# 9.    Recommended Links

**www.airsoftohio.com**

**http://www.airsoftohio.com/forums/showthre
ad.php?t=23550&highlight=radio+communica
tions**

www.theairsoftbible.com

# 10.  Other Acknowledgements

Thank you to Tim Thomas for the Photos
Thank you to my wonderful wife for the
editing

Thank you for getting The Airsoft Bible: Book of Comm. Please visit the Airsoft Bible on the website or on Facebook!

Watch for other books in the series.

# www.TheAirsoftBible.com

*Do unto others, before they do unto you!*

# NOTES

# NOTES

Made in the USA
Columbia, SC
11 December 2017